Grey Linings

Grey Linings

hergreyside

ACKNOWLEDGMENTS

I must thank those that helped this dream transpire.
For my nearest and dearest always, my heart is forever your home, that you have helped build strong.
To the readers who hold my words with ardor, I am humbled in complete gratitude.
To the inspiring souls I have connected with in the Instagram and Twitter Poetry Community, you move and muse me daily. And to any prompts within these spaces that have sparked a piece to be woven.
To the Cover Designer, Clare McKeown, for her creative digital talent and our beautiful journey.
And to my Editor and Proofreader, Jo Sexton, for her guidance and wonderfully taming my relentless dance with punctuation.
I am still pinching myself that this book has blissfully become tangible.

I thank you all greatly and deeply xo

For my Stars,
That light up my universe.

CONTENTS

SEA 9

CLOUD 39

MOON 69

ASHEN 97

DOVE 125

SMOKE 159

To weave freely
The words we bleed
All for the soul
To breathe.

SEA

RESTLESS. DEEP. CALM

Why Grey?
Because I am neither
A blinding beacon
Or a dark mistress.
Not the light
Or the dark side.
I am all the shades in between,
The thoughts,
The wants,
The unspoken.

I am but a restless haze,
Silvery mirrored
From your steely gaze.
I am *the same* as you.

I live in the shades,
All the shades that epitomize me.

But the wild
Was born to burn
Ever through her veins,
For it is more a part of her
Than any given name.

You are a beacon to my path,
A lighthouse in my storms,
The shoreline to my sea,
And my favourite place to be.
And so I am homesick but of you,
As you are the embodiment
Of my loving, living home.

But to him,
She was far more than a feeling.
She was his lighthouse,
A shelter,
A beacon,
Evermore harboring him
Safely back to shore.

The touch never needed a name.
I knew you
Like the earth
When at long last kissed
By awaited rain.

You are the peace,
The storm,
And all that weathers in between.

Grey Linings

The shells crunched underfoot
Until the sea lapped
To kiss my toes,
Sinking to ankles
Into the cool of salted foam,
And how I needed this,
To slip into an ocean dream,
While I sit here under sunset sky,
To greet each wave dissolving
As I goodbye the day
And sigh.

Let me run barefoot
By a sea
By home.

I ebb and flow
To shore as I please,
Your fishermen's folly
To hook in flesh,
Or need,
Is sadly wasted upon me.
I am no fish to satisfy a hunger.
I am the slipping,
Drifting,
Fluent sea.
'Tis only a captain of my choosing
That may sail,
May explore,
And have command of me.

I am by no means
Anyone's possession,
For how can you ask that of a storm?
You cannot possess
What is lightning, hail and thunder,
Hidden in human form.

You're mistaken.
I am not another many river.
I am an ocean that reaches
Beyond all others reach.

And what more could you ask
From a wild gypsy heart,
Whose love licks with flame
To engulf you whole,
Before they must dance on wind
With feet that were never bound
To grace ground long.

I need this rain, this pour
To cool down the heat
Burning, raging within my core.
I will consume myself
With what I burn
If I do not stand in its deluge
And let it wash its hardest,
To pound its drown of fire
Licking from each pore.
To pool not smoke,
Not ache,
A reprieve,
A break.
Please, just pour.

I am chaos
When peace needs claim,
For fire to feel rain.

Grey Linings

You'll have to excuse me.
The rain won't stop falling,
And thunder keeps calling my name
Home.

I am a saudade sea,
An endless lost,
Awash
In sunken melancholy,
To drift with pull
And churn with yearn
On tempestuous tides
That crash,
Colliding,
To always subsiding,
Waving at but the want
Of any other shore destiny,
To ever bottomless be
An empty vast, void body.
I am a saudade sea.

Just a shell of a thing,
Echoing the sea,
Of the wild creature
That once lived inside of me.

I won't lie
About my tidal soul.
I am tides upon rocks,
Still breaking smooth,
Crashing to claim
My something to prove.
I am spread as far as the eye can see,
With a mind still searching horizons.
I am sunken shells that still have songs
That can move like a siren's call.
I seek my still
To float and flow, drifting in the calm.
But how winds will have their churn
To rip ripples across my surface.
I have depths that I do not even dare to seek,
With monsters that have no name
Except for what they call me.
I am an ocean
And most won't handle the sea.
Some are better to leave
Their two feet on the sand
But how I wish you would dive
To meet me in my deep.

We are but made of sea
You and I,
Two the same
Flowing endlessly.

Bodies of water.

Not a little fish
Nor a big fish.
Simply a siren,
Also shipwrecked
In this unforgiving sea.

It was never just about you,
With your mighty wings you soar.
With my tail anchored to this sea,
You and I
Were never meant to be.

Tomorrow I won't be here anymore.
I'll have drifted back
To my ocean sea
That calls to me
With each felt wave,
Lapping at my heavy feet,
Ebbing my need to float,
To free.

Wild, calm or untamed,
Be as the ocean loves the shore.
Curl into me,
Lap my edges.
I'll meet your might
Relentlessly,
Always
Returning.

Hold me
In the way the shore enwraps
The silver lined sea.

A dressing down
By wild roars.
The ocean, *my ocean,*
Calls.

Calm the chaos,
Silence the waves,
Tame these surging seas
In me.

My Poseidon, your ocean in need.

There are oceans
You taste on her lips,
Secrets of depths
To pull you under,
A rip past shallow steps -
You're drowning in a kiss.

Bring about peace
In this restless sea
I whisper and softly bite his ear.

Imagination dripped
From the pores of her skin,
Pooling into poetry
Of drowning perfection.

*And thankfully
I never learnt how to swim.*

I am lost
In your wild seas
And I've never felt
So calm.

I feel only peace.

She was more a body
Of oceans
And galaxies
Than that of flesh
And bones.

Grey Linings

Can you paint me,
My lover?
In all my weird and wonderful.
With all my cracks and flaws.
For how you so beautifully
See this world,
One can only selfishly dream
Of how you may see me
Through those artist's eyes,
Never more, more seen.

The art I gaze at
Lovingly most,
Always lost in,
Is you.

Are we not all poets
When read by one
Who truly loves the depths of us?

If I am a song,
It is only when sung
Through your sweet voice
That I come most alive.

On lazy days
Like slow Sundays,
We sip on Earl Grey,
Floating
In a sleepy, dream state.
Records spin,
Redding and The Stones
With volume set to max.
We recite Edgar
And Blake
Over politics
And pandemics.
We kiss,
Feel,
Fool,
Fornicate,
Grazing on croissants
And lemon sugar pancakes.
On lazy days
Like slow Sundays,
We truly relax.

I will need you
To be my cup of coffee,
To drink you in slow
In each new morning light.

Coffee lovers.

You are homemade,
The best of that tenderly,
Self-made magic.
Like a homemade jam
Or that slice of homemade pizza.
A homemade card
Or a homemade sweater
With love stitched
Into the very seams
Of the softest sleeves.
And I love the coziness,
That unmatched warmth,
Of you,
Of my favourite made home.

Within two arms
Lies my home.

I tilt my head,
Moving in musing motions
To view all the marbled marvel
Of your iridescent beauty,
Cast at every colourful, curving angle.

A lighter love,
Lit in brightened beacon shine.
I see you
And marvel,
Lifting other's to dazzling dreams.
You are a dream
To eyes nothing less
A sparkling splendor
To enliven harrowed heart
Within charcoaled chest,
And you say I'm the one
But it is ever you
And your luminescent love.

It is where it beats faster
In a thrill pumping tune,
Where it lulls to slow calm
Like a river flowing
To the open sea.
It is you + me.

Home is where the heart breathes.

I think I have felt you before,
And yet,
I have only just met you now.

Déjà vu of the soul.

And as always,
All that was needed
Was your arms to wrap around me,
To dance our dance by stars grace,
The familiar moody brooding music,
Drifting on heavy air
To meld us,
Lull us,
To trace our well-rehearsed steps
In this lasting love of us.

Myriad = The ways in which I love you.

Real passionate love
Is indeed like wild flames
That can't burn through enough fuel,
Impossible to tame.
But it is also an eye of a storm,
The haven at your center,
An endless ocean crashing,
Feeling peace in each pull, each surrender.
Anything without both hunger and peace
Is more passionate lust
Than real passionate love,
That once in a forever.

You're going to make me dig without even knowing.
To question depths I thought I had already excavated.
Levels that most won't ever touch. I know I will find
myself a better version from being kissed long by
your love. A love I've forever envisioned, but never
thought possible to grasp. A love I've always given to
others. An equal. *A soul-fulfilling love.*

I do not,
And will not,
Love lightly.
I come with all my utility
To meet your heart,
All in.
To learn your territories
And surrender lovingly
To the endless fight
Of us.

The only side I choose. Our side. All in.

He had
The kind of kisses
You drown in
Willingly
While floating
To safety.

Careful *big little heart*,
You beat too full,
Too fast,
That others
Not even yourself
Can catch you sometimes.

This heart runs rampant on full charge.

You might look like a human,
But you, my love, are not.
You are poetry itself
In all its perfection,
Craftily bound in mortal flesh
And held by bone.

You remind me
Without words
Of what my heart is capable of.

It was that face I loved the most.
It bore me only infinite pleasures,
In small but infinite ways.
Each line marked an album of stories,
Each curve a work of the softest art,
And no amount of time on this earth
Could fade that love,
Not in memory,
Not in its age.

Forgotten is a word
That will never know you.

There is only
One kind of gold
I care to accumulate
In loving hold
And it beautifully beats
Inside your chest.

The folds
Of us,
Like origami lovers,
Tucked carefully
Into the other
To create anew.

If we do not love
'Till we seep
Into each other's very core,
Then what are we even doing here?
What are we *(not)* living for?

Seep to deeper love levels.

The wild electricity
Held in the moment,
Intensely, idly.
A mere twenty-three millimeters
Magnetically between
You and I,
And our lips full
Of charged anticipation.

More is said
In the silent conversations
Between loquacious eyes.

To be lost in some moments,
Beyond return,
Is the only way to be.

Let's get lost together.

Here we go again
Getting all love drunk
On these sunlight kisses,
Insatiable grins,
And the way our eyes sparkle
For darker delights.

I'm not asking for anything
But presence,
Passion
And peace.

Those three P's.

MOON

BEACON, MAGICAL, HEAVENLY

We make wild chemistry,
Meld into mind blowing biology,
Defying known physics,
To kiss our astronomy
Between all the space
That matters.

She danced with stars
And drank with galaxies,
Made love under moons
And got dirty with the belts.
She pondered most on life
With radiating supernovas,
All while her heels
Never left her earth.

What is under my skin:
Spaces where passion meets galaxies,
Where flame merges with sea,
Where light is dark the same,
A whole, wild, free.
That is the aether, the energy,
That only *you* will know of me.

Revealing.

She would be your moon
If you would be her sun.

With earth to flourish at our feet.

Like a blue moon in September,
She stole the night
With her rare, tinted, azure shine,
All with the coming of spring,
South of the equator line.

He had galaxies
In those eyes
And I found myself
Floating, vastly lost,
Amongst the stars,
Often.

It was the way she saw the world,
Her kaleidoscope view:
It enthralled and dazzled
In a wonderous way
He had never
Breathtakingly
Known.

Even her scars
Were stars
In his eyes.

There has been no moon
Without the thought of you,
Since you taught me
Of its scars of youth
With seas of darkly parts.
And how it reminded you
Of me.

And I will love
The stars in you
Always,
Even when they burn
And fall
Goodbye.

I find solace
In the cosmic ceiling sea,
When I surrender to its majesty.
Like a hypnotic sighing effect
Of perspective relief, slipping free,
As I timelessly gaze
And simply,
Gratefully,
Breathe.

Lost somewhere
Between the pages,
To be found
Amongst the stars.

Charmed by the afterglow hour,
Drawn to dusk
In its delicate mottled hues,
Like a Monet moth
To the eventide entrance,
The stained aflame tangerine
Kissed by lilac linings,
Swallowed by seeping ink
Of midnight sparkling blues.

Oh, what magic sunsets do ever brightly do.

I want to see
The raw reflect
Of today's sunset
Meeting your own dazzle,
Dancing across your body,
Like a stained-glass window
Of skin emblazoned sky,
Casting you in cotton candy
As I caress each colour,
Taste each flavour,
Mixing a mess of us
As heavenly art, alive and at play.

Get me at dusk,
Sunset dripping down my back,
With stars already twinkling home
In these irises, veridian charged,
At a wild peace.
And who knows where
This night will lead us,
What places these dancing feet
Will gracefully,
Daringly,
Lift to.

Playful in the moonlight hour,
You bring the wine,
I'll bring the twinkling light.
To make you laugh,
To make me sing,
To be all the delicate, firing beauty
Life can possibly, beautifully bring.

Mulberry wine
In the moonlight
And the stillness
Of your gaze
Upon my trembles.

Flammable

And each night, she slinked back
To snug stars and mellow moon,
To dally and toil
In songs of her day
With hopeful highs and sighs
Of come what may,
Floating away
'Till dreams consume.

It's a dream she has
On her grey bucket list,
A dream of hot air
From a bird's eye basket nest.
She wants to soar
Amongst technicolor clouds,
Upon foreign shores,
In Cappadocia crowds,
Come Turkey's summer play,
Horizons ballooning,
I long to float away.

You will find me there one day.

When the world
Feels a little normal,
Let us portal
To those exotic shores,
Where my soul longs to pour,
Licked by sun,
To dance by moon
By the salt-soaked sea
As we sip
That sweet coconut spiced rum
Off each other's
Golden honeyed bodies.
To wander,
To freely explore
Once more.
Covid free.

There's always been
Something about
Those hidden alleyways
And you.

To kiss you
In hidden places,
Amongst cobblestone lanes.

I have not yet met,
In person,
The city of Paris,
And so, perhaps, I am yet
To have truly met myself.

She forever sang
On the inside
Of foreign shores
And boundless adventures,
Lost to the pleasures of exploring.

He was more,
Like the world touched him more,
And he knew exactly how to move to it,
How to sway to it,
Almost molding it himself.
And oh, how I wanted him to make me sway
And mold me just the same.

He was a wildflower
If a flower
He must be,
Ever to roam,
Ever to bloom,
Ever to perfume
The sweetest scent.
Not for vases,
Nor pluck,
Nor pick,
But just to be wildly
Kissed by sun
And shined by moon,
To grow rampant,
To be but free
As wildflowers simply,
Beautifully,
Must be.

If I were a house,
I would be conservatory green,
Lush, thriving,
Wild, surviving.
A sanctuary of a jungle,
An abandoned secret garden
Sheltering hope
Through doors of emerald eyes.

In my art,
I find me
Differently
Every time.

ASHEN

BROKEN. HAUNTING. REMNANTS

I have daisy jean pockets
Stuffed full of glittering hope,
Gumnut dreams,
Love buttons,
And kinky, dirty notes.
Yet if I squint real hard
With both eyes shut,
They appear turned out empty
With but lost coins of regret,
Holes of doubt
And never ever nopes.

She's all rain,
Wild storms on air,
And you crave the drench.
But she will need your sun,
Your light, your warmth,
After her fall
And during her descent.

Creating rainbows.

There's only light
In the heavy spaces
And I wonder why
I can't feel its warmth
When it's at the tip of my fingers.

I needed you more
In my depth's darkness
Than your light ever did of me,
Or cared to cast your light to see.
And now your beacon is blinking,
The shine swiftly sinking,
At the drift of the awakened sea.

I loved him
For all the words
He never said,
All the words
I imagined in my head
To fall from his lips,
But never actually did.

Grey Linings

I'm not in your ear
Yet you're still on my tongue.
What sense is this
When our eye's touch our souls
But we caution with the smell of fear?

No sense at all.

Do you see me for me?
Or are you another
That merely sees in me
What they want to see?
A mask I wear you made for me.
A façade, a ploy,
A ruse for subterfuge,
To fit some mold,
To be not I.
To be a tin can hollowed toy
That is stuffed full
Of your own dreams
And your own wants,
Stitched with selfish seams.
And then you say that I'm a dream,
The girl for you.
If only you knew,
Blind, fickle fool,
How to see past
Your own made mask.

Grey Linings

You sang me songs
Of other loves
While I grasped
At the very straws
We laid our heads upon.

And through no fault of your own,
Other than you held to your truth,
You stained my heart
Forever melancholy blue,
For it knew
It could never harbor you
Or your unwilling heart
In any part of mine.

I hate that you became a ghost,
Trapped in memories form,
When you were once to be my all.
And now, that version of you
Simply does not exist anymore.

Abandon me.
This course is set for
Wreck and sink,
To be buried
On oceans floor,
Drowned deep,
Past bitter broken brink.
Abandon me.
Captain, it's not your ship.
It's only the notion
Of title and legend treasure.
There's a whole wide ocean
To find new sails,
To harpoon hoist.
Abandon me,
For I walked the plank,
Already caught
In the sea's curse of me,
To churn and yearn
Endlessly,
To a self-siren's call,
A pirate's death for me.

The only ship I sink
Is **my** own
With an anchor of **self-doubt**
And my course set
To a horizon **of not enough**.

A pirate to myself, robbing my worth.

I have a room full of you,
But its never felt so vacant.

When did you check out?

You left
And the words I needed
Began sinking in
To take your place.

The sinking beyond feeling,
When the knowing dawns
That the change in you
Was that you couldn't,
Or maybe simply wouldn't,
Love the change in me.

Can a shadow
Ever truly love anything
But which that it is cast from?
I fear I am more shadow
Than bone,
Than flesh,
Than known.

You hold in sky,
Taming back the swells
That threaten their break,
Hopeful that salt will subside
And this anxious pounding
From deep inside
Will come to bay,
Come to obey,
Bow down to stop,
Ruining dreaded days
With wasted worry wound,
Uptight, as a gripping vice.
It's not nice
To live this way,
To have fear in the simplest of tasks
While others walk around,
So light and free
Of self-debilitating paths.
But I get that that's anxiety for you,
A sick shadow having its lead
While you take its pace,
With strings you slowly strung
Yourself in careful craft,
In what you thought
Was once a way to control
The simplest of tasks.

The words came out
Without invite
But loaded with need.
To be freed,
To be her therapy,
To shake the soul awake.

The ball rolled into the undergrowth
To hide amongst the cool of shade,
Nestling in the soft darkness,
A safe haven from life itself.
Perhaps no one would find it again.
Perhaps that was the plan all along.
For that tired ball is me
And I don't want to play fetch anymore.

What she fights with -
Torrents to drown,
Currents to clash,
Lurking in her murky depths.
A warrior of oceans
In her cockleshell crown
And conch cut dress.

The battles we conceal, in our shells.

I dress in the reality
And what my world needs of me,
Hanging up my wants
And needs
And most of my identity.
And *fuck* sometimes it hurts to breathe,
To be everything
For the ones you love
And failing miserably,
With no time
To
Just
Be
Me.

Who was she again?

I wear melancholy
Too heavy,
Like a cheap perfume,
At an expense
I dare use too much,
For if I know it is there
And expose it so,
How can it creep up
To scare me so lowly,
Ever the same again,
When it lingers like a bad smell
For all to get to know
More than myself.

Just a dress of melancholy
And a broken zip
That won't undo.

I have doubted myself
In this life so far,
More than I have given
Myself praise.
It has become a daily chore in ways,
Always at the top of the list.
And I missed the patterns
Where I made this normal,
Where the habit of falling short
Became how I measured myself.
But I'm tired of it,
I'm tired of emptying my own bucket,
Filling my world around me
And never deeming myself worthy
Of being full IN myself.

I sit here
With my ghosts.
I write
And my pen
Brings them back
To life again.

I often make my bed
In the ghosts
Of past versions I've been,
And how it hollows me
To cling to these things
No longer seen
Or not meant to be.

Still learning to let go of self-ghosts.

Just blue jeans
Seeking the rip,
A carefree mark,
The tell-tale sign
Of lived.

Grey Linings

The earth
Feels heavy
Under feet
That need to fly.

These wings of mine,
Long folded in,
Need to stretch,
Need to beat,
Need to soar
The open skies again.

The power you hold
To weave your world
Has never left you from inside.
It just got a little buried
And fell asleep for a while.

You're already a diamond.
Stop pressurizing yourself.

Don't say
You are enough
Or *more than enough.*
The word *enough*
Will always fall short,
Like mediocre insult to majesty
Say you are endless,
Beautiful and bountiful,
You are multitudes
Evolving.
You are more than others
Can dream to see,
And more than your thoughts
Allow you to be.
I hate the cliché,
The downright betray
Of the inferior failsafe,
Short sheeting,
Laud cheating,
Don't dare say
You are more than enough
Just say
You are more
Instead.

I am
And always was
More than what your glimpse
And opinion thought of me.

She was the pearl you didn't see.
Shaping,
Forming,
Illuminating,
To grow,
Morph,
And be cultured,
Yet uncultured,
Into who she was always going to be.

The iridescent pearl
In the depths of a titanic sea.

You are not
What your past
Reminds to define you.
You are -
What ever your future desires
And your present actions.

I am no more the person I once was
Than the soaring butterfly is
To its crawling former form.

Entire galaxies
Played upon her
Delicate wings
To which she beats
To her own dazzling dreams.

There is an unrest in you
That whispers my name,
Knowing my answer
Is already the echo
To its need.

Not everyone is made of fireworks
Or flames.
Some are made of soft filled sky,
Of floating feathers,
Or perfumed petals.
And yet, that does not make them
Any less explosive
On another person's life.

In my softness
Only strength exists.

The problem was never in my strength
Rather always in your perception of it.

Dismantle your walls,
You iron hearted fool.
I have no want
To break you further
For I am here
To service
Those harshly
Engineered
Wounds.

She will rip at your walls
With her gentle touch
And formidable kind.

For she speaks with gentle love
And fireworks lit to burn.

Be the love that they know,
The light that won't falter,
The laughter that lifts
And their safety ever after
They remember.

A parent's love.

I am young hands
With eagerness,
An old heart
With missing beats.
A sharpened mind
Away on dream,
A sunshine soul
At peace, in the rain.

We collect moments
To stuff our minds,
Holding permanent, tight,
Dancing with them
To help define us,
To help remind us,
To help entice us
That this life is worth living.
Because such moments
Made it all worthwhile,
Made us sweetly smile
And must matter more
Then those that broke our being.

YOU

ARE

THE

MOMENT.

Own your time.

We took moments
And showed them
How to be unforgettable.

If I must do it on my own,
Make no mistake,
I will.
For the mountaintops
Already hear my name
And the fires know
I was born of the same,
And the oceans call me kin,
Knowing they are my home.

There is a pounding
To my purpose,
A piercing
In its need,
A ringing to its call,
A hunting hunger
I must feed.

My only wish
Is to manifest
What my heart truly sings for,
Yearns
In songs of want and longing for,
Dreams that must be more
With tangible end,
Felt with grasp
But released in final peace
Of complete,
Of happened,
Of the end I must one day meet.
To look in the eyes of
And reside
In sighing
At last relief.

Let us spew art from our veins
And let go of inhibitions,
With caution pelted at winds
And a *snap, crack* of breaking reins.
Be as wild as your core that burns
Like a furious furnace flamed.
That is you
And your soul
And the very effect you transcend
Into existence.
Let it out.
Let it all *fucking* out
And pour from pen
To universe.

To stress less
About the bloom,
The *if*
Or the *when,*
And focus on the growing
And knowing your **why.**

Grey Linings

Stop looking for the silver linings.
Look for beauty in the dove,
In the ashen,
The sea,
And the plain, everyday
Grey.

For linings
Come in all shades.

Sometimes there is no silver lining -
It's just all grey
As far as the heart can feel for now,
And that's okay too.

Grey skies
Never cloud the fall
But pour a chance
To grow.

I want my words
To be stored on shelves,
In boutique bookstores
By dressed up windowpane.
To seep in souls
And move in muse.
To flitter hope.
To hug in rhyme.
To be quoted with ardor.
To help someone's cause.
To weave such words,
Such words,
That so rule my very all.

Conspire
To inspire
Beautiful things.

She's doing life
The only way she knows,
Dancing with the fire,
A flower behind her ear,
Rolling in the leather
With starlight in her eyes,
In her seas, after storms.

I want to fall in love
A little more each day ...

With my life.

Madly & truly.

A day without poetry,
Written, read or thought,
Is indeed, for I,
Not a day in itself
Yet felt.

You may live life softly,
Or hard at it,
But either way,
Live it always
With incessant passion.

Feed life passion.

SMOKE

MESMERISING, INTOXICATING, BREATHTAKING

That cool autumn wind
Sneaking in
To goosebump cheek
And thighs
And thoughts within.

She's poetic spitfire
That revels in the rain
With the sting of poisoned petals
To ignite passion with pure arcane.

You existed between the spaces,
The air felt
But never seen,
A curious thing
Like an aura
That the eyes lack to capture,
But the heart claims its keep,
And how my mind played with you
In maddening curiosity.

Let me slip into something
A little more comfortable,
Like your mind.

I consume your words
To taste your mind
When I cannot have your mouth.

If I cannot have your lips,
Let me have this,
The place where I crave to pour my poetry
And to taste and inhale yours.

The sacred crescent of your neck.

You baptize me
In that sweet spot,
My tilt back weakness
That brings me to my knees
Between earlobe
And collarbone.
The rest is always a blurring mess,
Lost in your heavenly unknown.

My neck and your magical lips,
Who am I to stop such a spell as this?

There is sunshine
Kissing our skin
Gently
As we with curious lips
And hungry hands
Are lost
In our own sweetness,
Slowly soaking each other in.

Let me slowly undress the day
Before I slip into your night
And you tell me to stay.

My favourite place
To take a seat
And admire the view
Is upon your lap
Between each
Syncopating
Breath.

When you can't get them
Off your tongue;
When it tastes like
Forever.

Taste me,
Consume me,
Drink every last delicious drop
Of the passion you cause
In what we havoc,
In our passionate wild,
With longed lost laws.

This love,
Lapping gently,
To lick our souls from wounds
With the sweetest amor.

If you make me beg,
I'll bite my lip
And do that thing
That makes your blood run wild,
Just to see
Who gives in first.

I feel your tug,
Your rip,
Your pull,
At my lulling
Salt sea back.
You call to come,
Moon Master above,
A call I cannot deny,
For it is in my nature
To be your sea
And move as you so command of me.

Eyes never looked so compelling,
Tasted as stoking, provoking
As his stare
When I undressed
Like the autumn fall -
Burning, turning
Into something on fire.

Ignite this body with your touch,
Set fire to this longing lust,
Flames licking skies to stars.
Let's burn this night to its dawn.

Let's see if our shadows
Can keep up
With our flames.

Let us move,
Smooth,
Silken,
Through our desires,
Dark Art
In the dark.
Neon lapis blue,
Low lighted room,
Swoon,
Playing
The roles we choose
For each other's musing.
Pleasures
Conjured,
Conducted,
Instructed and new
As we sip each other's
Ambrosial appeasing brew.

Might I invade your dreams?
Pirouette on in
To be the muse to your needs.
A honeyed hourglass,
Pouring to please,
Making make believe stand still
While I'm down on my knees.
To be a carnal canvas
In a mixed media of binds
For your artistic expertise.
Come, make messy dreams
Out of me.

I want to rock
My hips
To the rhythm of the storm,
Feeling each rumble you make
Between my legs.
Screaming out to the heavens
As thunder blankets
The hellish sounds from our bed.
Heavy felt, pelting wet.

I want to be that little storm
Between your clever hands.

Tell me how it feels
To move my architecture
From the belly of need
To understand both our designs
And capabilities.
To kiss flame
And not bleed
But feed for more,
For the insatiable build
'Till freed.

I want to move with you
In the way that you need,
The way that I need:
The give and take
In the heat of all that we are
And all that we can be,
A love that riddles
Within our veins,
Licking purpose
In endless flames.

In all of myself,
In all of yours
An equal claim,
An equal surrender.

There's no right or wrong
Between us
In this intimate,
Infinite space.
This moment among moments,
It's just ours.
Just us.
And oh, how intoxicatingly
We make it firing glow.

The base of my spine
Where dimples pool
Knows your name
Like my hips
That hiss yes
For the encore.

The taste of earth, salt
And whiskey travels
Still lingers on his lips
And I am infatuated
With exploring
Each and every adventurous kiss.

You taste of adventure,
Sweet pleasures,
And no regrets.

You tell me
To be a good girl,
To focus
And spell out my name,
But I always lose it
And let go
At the final 'O'
That's not even in my name.

My favourite lessons.

You cause ripples upon this flesh,
Vibrations deeper
Under liquid surface,
And so I beg for more stones
To cast,
To skip,
To cause
And effect
My stirring stillness,
To uncontrollably lap and flow
In coursing, rhythmic succession
And watch what you make me do.

You ebb, I'll flow.

You come to me
In dream
With lustful hands
And I bend the knee,
Surrendering
To the pleasure
Of each other;
To our thirsting needs.

Let the blackest straps,
Lace back up
Thoughts that tickle
To tease my bite,
And crimson claws retract.
For it is only me tonight
With the wine,
Alone in this bed.

Sweet vivid reverie.

You cannot quiet the passion
Nor shame its cause to spread,
For love in its intensity
Is what we breathe,
We bleed,
We live,
And die *(with a smile)* for.

Live your wild
Love your most.

READ MORE *hergreyside* VIA:

Instagram: @hergreyside_

Twitter: @HerGreySide

TikTok: @hergreyside_

Facebook: @HerGreySideQuotes

ABOUT THE AUTHOR

hergreyside is Kira Legge, an Australian Poet, born and raised on the East Coast of Australia. Known as Grey of hergreyside, she writes modern poetry that comes from all the different shades of everyday living. Floating between the black and white and all the thoughts in between. She is a wife and mother to three little stars, a lover of forests, the sea and all that is poetry, in all its forms.

Grey Linings

Copyright © Kira Legge 2022. All rights reserved.
No part of this book may be reproduced, distributed, downloaded or transmitted in any form or by any means, including photocopying, recording, or other mechanical methods, without prior written permission of the author and publisher.

This edition first published in 2022

ISBN: 979-8-8365-8713-0

Editor and Proofreader - Jo Sexton
https://www.facebook.com/josextoneditor

Cover Designer - Clare McKeown - Instagram: @c.m.poet

Printed in Great Britain
by Amazon